SUPERMARKET

by Kathleen Krull

illustrated by
Melanie Hope Greenberg

Holiday House / New York

To my partner-in-groceries, Paul
K. K.

To Key Food, Brooklyn Heights, New York,
and a melange of thanks to:
Donald, Enrico, Israel and Ivan,
Anna "Arugula" Kelly, Barbara "Chef-Girl-Ardee" Yvinne,
Darlene, Fred, George, Joan, Joyce, Julia, Martin,
Modesta, Muhammed, Omar, and Ruth
M. H. G.

Text copyright © 2001 by Kathleen Krull
Illustrations copyright © 2001 by Melanie Hope Greenberg
All Rights Reserved
Printed in the United States of America
The text typeface is Barcelona.
The medium of the artwork is gouache.
www.holidayhouse.com
First Edition

Library of Congress Cataloging-in-Publication Data
Krull, Kathleen.
Supermarket / by Kathleen Krull;
illustrated by Melanie Hope Greenberg.
p. cm.
Summary: Explains modern supermarkets and how they work,
discussing how they organize, display, and keep track
of the items they sell.
ISBN 0-8234-1546-5
1. Supermarkets—Juvenile literature.
2. Supermarkets—United States—Juvenile literature.
[1. Supermarkets.] I. Greenberg, Melanie Hope, ill. II Title.
HF5469.K76 2001

381'.148'0973—dc21
99-088042

Shopping carts clang.

Magic doors whiz open and shut.
Colors glow under bright white lights.
So many breakfasts, lunches, and dinners!
It's all at a special, necessary, very real place:
the supermarket.

The supermarket is a whole world of its own. Where does all this crunchy, munchy, sweet, sour, fiery, frozen, fabulous food come from?

ON SALE

SPECIALS

The doors don't really open by magic. When an electric "eye" overhead "sees" you coming, it starts a motor to open the doors.

GOURMET FOODS

sugar/salt/ cake mix

JUICE & SODA

OATS & MORE

According to surveys, shoppers decide in their first 8 seconds whether they feel comfortable in a store. The first thing they see helps them decide.

GOODS

CEREAL

milk
milk
milk
milk
milk

Happy Farms

Certain states are famous for certain foods: Iowa for popcorn, Vermont for maple syrup, Michigan for cereal, Wisconsin for cheese, Idaho for potatoes, Massachusetts for cranberries, Florida for oranges, California for grapes, Georgia for peaches and peanuts.

It all begins on farms.
Our food comes from places with lots of sunshine, rich soil, and clean water. Farmers make decisions every day during the long months of growing.

At harvesttime, workers pick the fruits and vegetables.
They pack everything neatly in boxes and load the boxes
onto trucks.

Picking fruits and vegetables
can be painful, low-paying work.
César Chavez (1927–1993)
became a hero for workers
when he founded the National
Farm Workers of America.

Small trucks, big trucks, gigantic trucks—
all rev up their engines.
Every night, drivers take off from farms or warehouses.
They zoom down the highway toward your town.

Among many other foods, American Indians introduced to the rest of the world chocolate, potatoes, tomatoes, beans, peppers, and, most important, corn. Some form of corn appears in more supermarket foods today than probably anything else.

In early America, most people were farmers. American Indians taught the new arrivals what to grow.

Families grew all their own food.
Later, they traded food with one another
to get other things they needed.
They started using money to buy things
at town marketplaces.
Soon there were general stores
where you could buy almost anything...

and little, family-run grocery stores—"mom-and-pop" stores. Stores became bigger, dividing items into different departments.

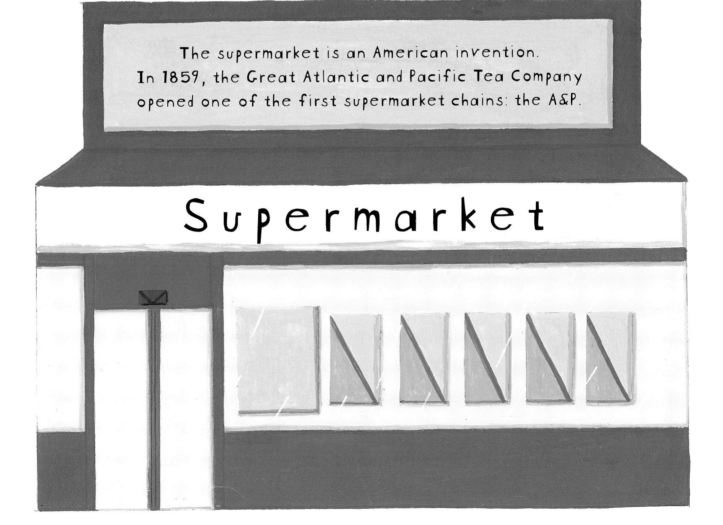

The supermarket is an American invention.
In 1859, the Great Atlantic and Pacific Tea Company opened one of the first supermarket chains: the A&P.

One potato chip company uses a giant
computer in Texas to keep track of every
bag of chips sent to every store every day.
At midnight, the computer
tells how many bags
of chips need to be
delivered to each
store the next day.

lettuce
lettuce
lettuce

CUPS

NEW

CUPS

CUPS

TODAY
ONLY

Now we have an amazing place where
every morning workers have a whole
"super" market all ready for you.
They have unpacked thousands of boxes and
arranged everything on the shelves, just so.

THE FOOD PYRAMID

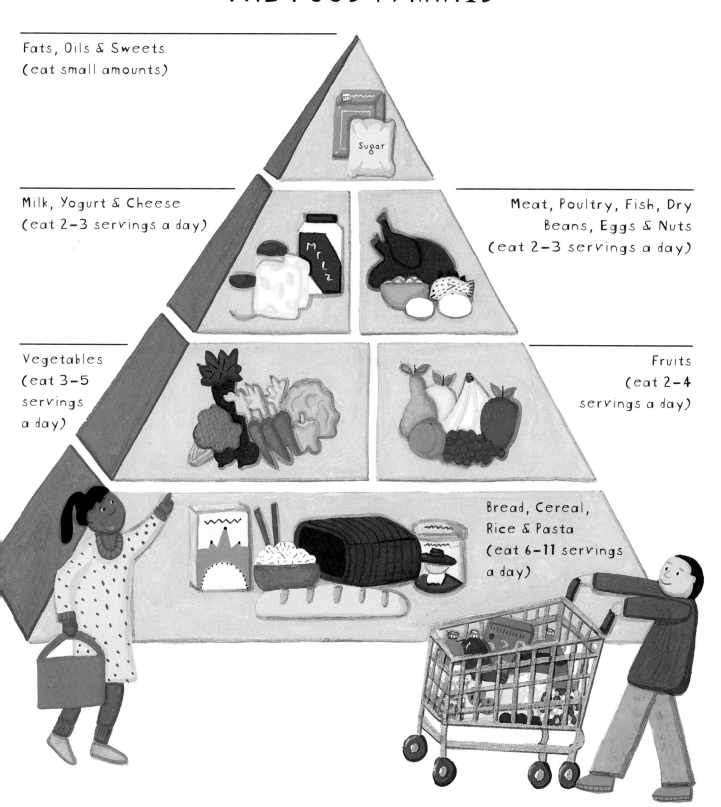

Fats, Oils & Sweets
(eat small amounts)

Milk, Yogurt & Cheese
(eat 2-3 servings a day)

Meat, Poultry, Fish, Dry
Beans, Eggs & Nuts
(eat 2-3 servings a day)

Vegetables
(eat 3-5
servings
a day)

Fruits
(eat 2-4
servings a day)

Bread, Cereal,
Rice & Pasta
(eat 6-11 servings
a day)

Some kids might think of the supermarket
as the place that sells candy.
But sweets are just a small part of what we eat.

You can find more variety in the fruit and
vegetable section than anywhere else:
fresh, juicy, strange, familiar.

Bananas are the most popular fruit, followed by apples, watermelons, oranges, cantaloupes, grapes, grapefruits, strawberries, peaches, and pears.

SPECIAL

Shoppers look, touch, sniff, compare, weigh—
and watch out for automatic sprayers.

Beds of crushed ice keep the meats and fish fresh.
Butchers cut or grind meat into different sizes and
wrap packages in plastic.

B-B-Q

For most of human
history, food has often
spoiled before it could
be eaten. Not until the
1800s did people learn
how to preserve food by
sealing it inside metal
cans. Around 1830, the
English figured out a way
to chill their food with
machines.

According
to surveys, the top
reasons why shoppers pick
a particular store are:
1. location,
2. prices, and
3. selection.

SALE

MANAGER'S SPECIAL

The best smells float around the bakery.
Bakers sometimes bake thousands of doughnuts
a day and at least a dozen different kinds of bread.

Just about everyone stops in the dairy section.
Behind all the eggs, milk, yogurt, and cheese
is a refrigerated area keeping everything cold.

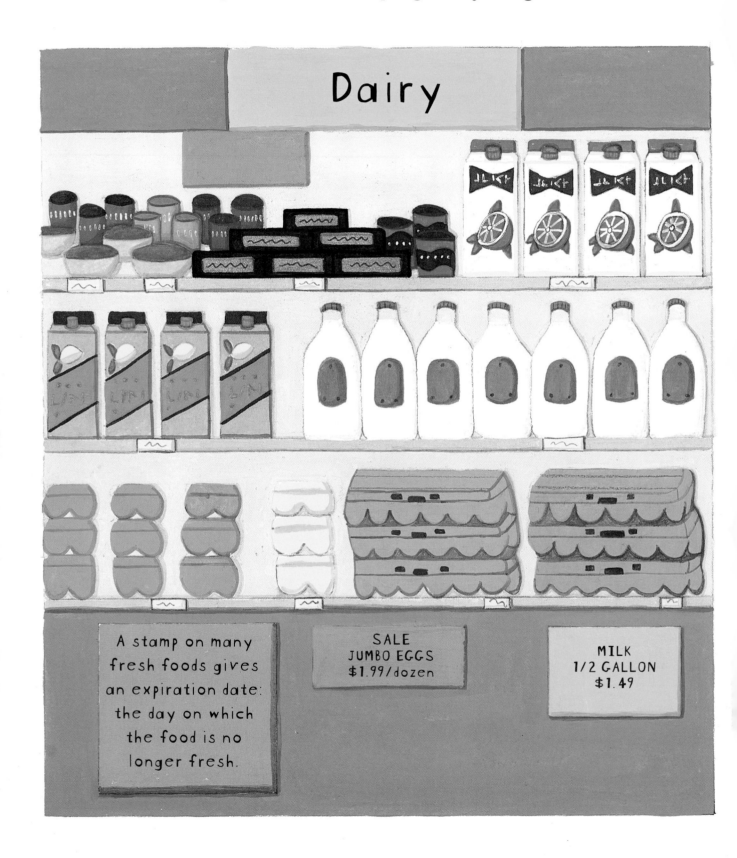

By far, the most popular flavor of ice cream is vanilla. Other favorites: chocolate, butter pecan, strawberry, chocolate-chip cookie dough, cookies and cream, and cherry.

APPLES
$1.99 lb.
69¢
GRAPES

JUICE
99¢
$1.89
SODA

EGGS
$1.99
$149 dozen
BUTTER

FROZEN FOODS

COUPON SPECIAL

NEW

A sweater is handy in the frozen foods section, where the air is coldest. Zippy music makes some people hum along or dance right in the aisle.

If you lined up all the boxes of macaroni and cheese sold each year, the line would stretch from Los Angeles to New York and back again—more than 9 times.

What is a "nonfood"? Something in a supermarket that we don't eat—like toilet paper, laundry soap, toothpaste, shampoo, and magazines.

The store is packed with cereal, soups, spices, and even "nonfoods."

At the checkout counter, people try to pick the shortest line. An electronic scanner "reads" the bar codes on most products and prints out the prices. A cash register adds up the cost of your food. Baggers ask "Paper or plastic?" and pack up your groceries.

Think about all the people who move food from the farms to your kitchen shelves!

The average wait in the checkout line is 8 minutes.

Even more goes on behind the scenes.
Managers keep track of inventory, their supply of foods.
Using computers, they find out what is selling
and order more for the trucks to deliver.

There are stockrooms with food ready to be moved
onto empty shelves; bathrooms for the workers;
a room where they eat their lunch;

a place for garbage, damaged products, and spoiled food; a place where boxes get unloaded;

and a place where empty boxes get recycled.

And cleaning supplies.
No one wants to see a hint
of dirt or germs at the supermarket.

The supermarket has row after row
of colors, shapes, and words that shout.
Some kids learn how to read right here,
from signs, labels, and shopping lists.
The supermarket is a good place to
practice math, too.

pet
food

MANAGER'S
SPECIAL

household cleaners

bleaches and deterg

2 for $4

3 for $5

THIS WEEK
ONLY
3 for $3

NEW
4 for $3

NEW

1/2
price

SPEC
2 for

half price

12 oz.
for $2

Mu   Mu   Mu

Mu

SPECIAL

3 jars for $5

express
10 items
or less

coupons

8 lbs.
for $5.99

Americans spend more than **$440 BILLION** a year at our supermarkets.

4 oz. $1.99

5 oz. $2.49

COUPON SPECIAL

COUPON SPECIAL

SALE

3 gallons for $4.99

NEW

MANAGER'S SPECIAL

ENJOY

6 oz. $1.79

Over half of shoppers, especially women, use a shopping list to make sure they don't forget anything. The average shopping list contains 22 items. Still, over half of what shoppers buy in a store is not on their list.

A supermarket helps us celebrate holidays
and big moments in our lives.

The supermarket even helps us know who we are. Are we the kind of person who likes macaroni and cheese in a box? Or spaghetti in a can? Orange juice or grape juice? Peanut butter: smooth or crunchy? Definitely pizza, but what kind?

The average family visits a supermarket more than twice a week. The average trip takes 45 minutes. Shoppers with children (more than half) spend more time and money. Companies try hard to figure out what shoppers want to buy; they even want to know what kids like. They design packages meant to appeal especially to kids—for items like cereal, cookies, and soft drinks.

Racing carts is not allowed. Begging for treats makes parents crabby.

Shopping for groceries is a super family time, deciding which things to pile in your cart.

Every family has to go—week in, week out.
The supermarket helps to shape the lives of everyone.

The supermarket is never quite the same from day to day. New items are added all the time, especially from around the world. Some markets have other stores right inside—worlds of their own.

Supermarkets are always changing.
Now some people order groceries
right on the Internet,
without even leaving the house.
But the supermarket will always be around—
one place that is never boring,
a very real place like nowhere else.